O For the Love

Vivian Kearney

ISBN-13: 978-1-63065-142-8

PUKIYARI PUBLISHERS
www.pukiyari.com

Thanks to Milo, my dear husband, our supportive families, and our very helpful editor, Ani Palacios.

Dedicated to all care receivers and caregivers

Index

Starting With

At First

God and Adam walking together
Identified every being
So happy were these to be named
That together they harmoniously
Wove Eden

Advice to Eve

Stop before the intake
After it will be too late
And you'll miss God

Birth, Creation

She gave birth
And she saw
How marvelous the baby was
And fell in love
With the newborn's loveliness

God created
The day and night
The stars and lights
Plants and animals
Earth and seas

And He saw
How good it was
And He loved
His creation
In its loveliness

Freshly Woken

With the
New dawn light
Waking the eyes
Like freshly fallen snow

Without the
Day's mistakes, gravity's regrets

Let my thoughts, words, feelings
Worship Thee, Father

Will It Be

Streaming poetry, will you keep flowing
Chasing thoughts, don't run so fast
Search for identity, will you look out the window
To pray for others and strength for tasks

Let the flowers outweigh the clouds
Let thanks outrun bitterness
Let's minister and be ministered to
May all God's many splendored names bless

Literary Quandaries

Literature with its catharses
Warmth and evoked sympathies
Proposes though doesn't answer
Real world questions of weary travellers

Their problems can remain unresolved
Until the amazing discoveries in actuality
Of the Bible's answers to literary quandaries
God's letters reassuring us graciously

Write What You'd Like to Read

The book that I would like to read, write
Need to read, write

Would acknowledge
Every thought auto
Each burdened with worries car
Trapped in my mind's
Circular race track

And would pray with me
Asking God to drive
Creating a passage
And a more linear road

For a learning pilgrimage
An easier journey
To meet our Father

Allow God

Fearful of loneliness
Clinging to groups
That suspect
Foreign infiltration

Run to solitude's
Beatitudes

Allow God
To sweeten
Your sour thoughts

And let your projects
Be your approving friends

Hibernating Healing Projects

Photos of the past, recaptured
Smiles of moments gone by
How were we so young, so healthy
And where are
Yesterday's radiant skies

Tactical, Strategic, Present, Future

The impulsive
Haphazard life

Tactical, not strategic
Often not tactful

When the future is held hostage
To the mesmerizing present

Though it's not so resolving either
To completely hand the present
And its marvels over
To the feared future

Various Alphabets for Hallelujahs

Thou art Alpha and Omega
Dear Abba

From A to Z
Be praised
Worshipped and prayed to
Aleph to Tov

Keep us using
Various alphabets
To send Thee hallelujahs

Prayer

The poems have revealed
Our itineraries, trajectories, train tracks
Their metaphors speaking God's language
While His hands dry our tears, lead us

The dreams have often been
A partly legible Rosetta stone
Their messages veiled in wispy ciphers
Clues to quandaries briefly shown

Death and illness, power and fear
Have bullied their way into many a kingdom
Lord, please defend, protect, lead each life
Please light every step to Thy salvation

Our Nature, Needs

Yet We're Here

If we didn't have shadows
We wouldn't be three-dimensional souls

If we weren't walking wounded every day
We might not care to help or pray

If we were marvelously perfect and wise
We would still be tripped by our egos' lies

If it weren't for our creating and saving God
We wouldn't be here wondering at all

Please Advise

For
All my shortcomings
And shortness, Lord

Thou dost advise
Compensations, adjustments

Please let me listen
And gratefully follow

Ghrelins

The grazing, growling ghrelins
Have me under their spell

I eat, then realize remorsefully
Plans for
Digestion and weight
Moods and metabolism

Have now regressed and
Are not doing very well

False Friends

Trojan horses come crashing
(Food promising healing and happiness)
Through forests of our neuroses

Flat or Nuanced

Black and white, flat and gray
Two-dimensional we observe
As we meet, consider others

Though ourselves, o how nuanced
Multilayered, complicated
Intricate and rainbow colored

It's An Expression

– I'm good
Decline many
Politely

– Are you sure?
Didn't you know
That's an impossible statement

Given the bent
Of human nature

Yearning

Mentsch
To try
To become

But never
Can we
Totally be
That perfect
Or good

Since that is reserved
For God
Who became a *mentsch*

Kind and considerate
Wise and gracious

One and only
Divine and holy

Though we can yearn
For human perfectability

Job and Us

Are we all Job's friends
Kind of people
And not really Jesus' companions?
Do we base our vaunted views
On wrong perceptions, premises?

Where is our brotherly love
In this many-neighbored world?
What happened to the dove above the church
Symbolizing God's Holy Spirit?

Let us all truly be Jesus' friends
In good fellowship, understanding and helpfulness
May all step out of their fortified tribal camps
And for God's wondrous works, attributes
His holy name honor and bless

Just Trying

Don't other me
With your wall of hate
Bricks of criticism

I'm just trying to walk
Another fine line
Build my own ladders

To discover a positive path
To see, follow and keep
A good and considerate
Trajectory

Seeds, Weeds and Walls

Maybe we are alike, you and I
With much more in common behind our walls

It's just what we do with the seeds and weeds
Of seeming discordance that may lead

To missed communications
Disappointed expectations

If God would our souls from clanish strongholds release
We could build a sweetened, bridging peace

Winds of Change

Algorithmic habits
Ingrained natures

You did this, saw this
This way before
Nags your mechanistic core

And that was perceived, followed
Traditionally
By our families, society
Need to keep it going
Infinitely

But those pesky viruses mutate
Winds of change
Can move viewpoints, customs
Residential fates

And there we are
Breathing under a foreign star

Speaking, Writing

A dance
With words
Back and forth comments
I learned to exchange
In a cultural art
Of conversation
Many years ago

Now continues
Too automatically

Acerbic
Critical
Cynical
Challenging
Argumentative
Pessimistic

Whereas
The writing
Tries to move
Across the page
With hopefulness
Consideration, inspiration
Faith and optimism

For better
Together days
How to
Tame the talk
Think before I speak
Learn more graceful speech dances

Let the fractal patterns
Of quick comments
Or lengthy discussion
Model kindly smiling flowers
And upwardly branched praying trees

Please Resensitize

Have we become so crassly desensitized
As ear cilia are frazzled by modern music, politics
That we don't allow our spirits to hear or see
The many miracles and messages sent tenderly

God of our fathers, mothers, sisters, brothers
Who walked us through wars,
Slavery, deserts and the Red Sea

Wouldst Thou also talk to us, counsel, heal, lead us
Resensitize our perceptions,
Wonder, empathy, speech and trust

Need a Hand

I, myself and my shadow
Need to protect me and mine
Though bootstraps are too distant to pull up
And it's impossible to watch my back

Who can untangle our sorrows
Who can reason with the nonchalant
Only God knows when and how
To save, to heal, to lend a (wounded) hand

What We Aren't

I am not
We are not

The Teacher, Preacher
To fulminate, debate, subordinate
Tendencies, privacies

We can only pray silently
For others' good balance, courage
And our own

I See, Sadly

– So, I see, sadly
You have
A splinter in your eye
That hinders
Your vision
Here, let me help you
Take it out

What's that I hear?
What is it
That Jesus is saying?

– Yours are as painful
Or worse
Seventy times
Seventy thousand splinters
Forming two sinister beams

– No, can't be …

No In Our Nature

No before yes
Yells the toddler
Finding language, voice

No before yes
Chooses the teen
Seeking place, identity
Fulfilment, road, cohorts
And mentors

No before yes
Declared the new nation
Under thoughtful construction
Trying to establish solid values
Wisdom, equitable government
For all

No instead of yes
Should have said Eve
To misleading temptation

No before yes
Should each grown person
Remember when confronted
With power hunger
And other devotion-demanding idols

.....

All veils masking God's quiet questions
Seeking a yes

– Do you love Me?
Will you feed My sheep?
Will you help, empathize with your neighbors
On their pilgrimage?

– Yes, I want to, yes I will
With my whole
Mind heart and soul
Though will I be able?
We wonder

Yes, says God
I will give you
Strength and grace,
Place, identity, good neighbors, mentors
Voice and My Holy Spirit's counsel

For your needed road

Our Wonderful Will

Our beautiful will
Our vivacious volition
Our natural knowledge

That self-medicates through tests
That strives for lasting happiness
Unfortunately, sometimes
Falling into addiction's spells

How much more comforted, fulfilled
Would we be
Seeking, doing, following
God's healing plan for each minute, day, year
If only we had the will to hear

More or Less – Luke 5:4-6; John 21:6

So, you know how to fish
(More or less)
You know where they lurk
You can judge the time and the seas
When to cast your nets
How to hedge your bets

God knows better than you
The minor fishing and living details
The major missions, decisions and cares
Ask and let Him answer humbled prayers

Martha or Mary – Luke 10:38-42

Who should I be today
Martha or Mary?

Jesus please tell me

Can I borrow
A little
Of both ladies' skills?

Though it seems
Martha needed more of
Mary's type of attendance
In Jesus's presence

Overwhelming

Overwhelming
Emotions, commotions
Block reason, starve love

But without those insistent
Highs and lows
Can calming insights
Of poems flow?

High Hopes

Can we read others
As they would be read

Can we not enslave
Others to our idea
Of who they are

Can we refrain
From forcing neighbors
To see ourselves
As we do

Then, beyond,
Can we see the necessities
Beyond sensations

Can we detect order
Behind confusions

And can we perceive God
Above the windows
Of our sanctuaries

Merited Too

All homemakers should be recognized
At least with
Multiple scouting badges

One for cooking
One for cleaning
One for inventing pragmatic uses
For diverse objects
One for practical, healing skills
One for finding, enlisting
And accepting support
One for keeping traditions
One for crafting new traditions
And organizing safe adventures
One for remembering diverse interests

One for managing time
And balancing it all
Lovingly
Through and beyond
Adversity's grim calls

Attitudes, Beatitudes

I guess it's a spectrum
Curvilinear, rainbow-like

Bitterness at one end
Gratefulness on the other

And though we continue
Walking hopefully

Towards golden thanks
Treasures of happiness

We can slide back down
So quickly

To worries'
Parched and lonely ground

Many times a day
Or often

Within the space
Of several minutes

Outside the Box

Minister
Outside the box
Jesus pleaded

But we put Him
In many other ones

It's Natural

Cats and dogs
Want to be petted

Objects and surfaces
Need a caring dust cloth

Our bodies and hearts yearn
To be loved and loving

God asks
For more good walks and talks
With Him

Please Let Us Know

Is much dreamed of,
Needed heaven
In this universe
Or above?

Can we talk to Thee, God
Here with our faculties
Language and thoughts
Or only later?

Please tell us
Before we sleep
Help us abide with Thee forever
In faith and trust

Consider

A Real Possibility

Faith and reason
Should be friends
Walking together, discussing
Amicably

And not fight over
Separate territories
Possessively

Must It Always Be

Stone age, bronze age, iron age, technical age
Always hunting mammoths, ending fellow denizens
Heckling order, pecking order, bullying the scurrying
When will we cooperate
To build Thy peaceable kingdom

Memories of otherhood,
Neighborhoods not understood
That's where families cry, souls sigh today
Distant rainbows miraging
Monetary dreams of finding
Rooms of gold that would take us in from the cold

Endemic greed, physical and metaphorical pandemic
Has blinded and deceived many over-zealous saints
Who believed their own righteousness in following
Charismatic politicians waging war against reality

Lord, please give us brave backbones,
Ears, hearts, eyes
May miracles of awakening to truth and consequences
Dawn on our lands

Help these Thy creation and creatures
Follow Thy lamp of wisdom,
Thy footsteps of kindness

Hallevai (May It Be)
Democratic Convention 2020

Hallevai, we'll help you as you help us
Sail to a better version of our lands
With some baggage but also trust
That you will prove to be our good friends

We will vote for you as you vote for us
Moving the ship of state to justice and kindness
As we sigh *hallevai*, may it be and share we must
When we witness governing ideals at their finest

Let Us Move Towards Greater Unity

– Let's keep standing defiantly
With our golden leaders
Says the right – they will keep us warmly
In their family barricaded with bluster and privilege
Weaponized with hate, threats and fact-refusals

– Let's keep moving with our historical
And future hopes
Towards kind societies, cultures for this nation, world
Says the left – truth, acceptance,
And warm inclusion will bring
More long-lasting health, equity and happiness to all

Those Holocaust Trains of Hate

Those once and still used
Holocaust trains wait
On destruction's tracks
To flee from God's love

Viruses Gone Viral

We aren't considering enough
Various viruses gone viral
Such as the distracting other pandemic
Of corrupt and corrupting
Politicians, bandwagons, systems

For it appears that
The metaphorical aspect of Covid
Warns that our spiritual health
Is failing also

Idolatrous Bandwagons – 2021 – Matthew 24:24

Even if the wrongly persuaded
Can be shown to forego
Ragged clothes or world views

That aren't really right, reasonably
Nor match up logically
And never fit all that well

Most likely changing these
Fashions and minds publicly
Would not happen quickly or easily

In front of others who sadly
Warned their neighbors to reconsider
The dangers of political swaggering

May all those swags be discarded
Soon, before we're all forced to wear
The uniform conformity
Of fascism's cruelty

Effects

Cultures of Death, Holocaust

Auschwitz, camps, villages, ghettos revisited
Describe with sharpened pencil how it feels
To tour with tv documentaries the slaughter
Unspeakable

How some of those bleached corpses – pieces they
were called
Were piled, tallied, were your forever lost families and
their neighbors
Who couldn't escape evil unleashed, paying by the
millions
For their differing looks and / or ancestries

O for the love of God, caring Creator
May vaccines against deranged ideologies
Be found and accepted

Family, National Stories

Broken, lost
Family stories that can partially
Be reconstructed by an ancestry program

Reviving some past lives
Proving how connected
We always were, still are

Lately the political race
And breaking, cyclical news
Reveal revenge's fearsome faces
Racism's cruel claims to power
Resentful steps into hatred's volcanos

Lord, may decency, reason and kindness
Mercy and truth and wisdom
Be our guides to Thee

Thy love reign on this planet
Beneath the stars

Meeting Through Readings, Writing

After reading
Horrified about
The ghettos and the Holocaust

Writing poems
Are a two-way ticket
Back to the
Times, peoples, places
The lack of spaces, basics, kindnesses
The sufferings, cruelties, deaths

The return pass
For this time-machine express
Crumpled with
Survivor guilt

Orphan / Mother

You looked for your mother
Orphan child
You just found another orphan
Saddened and wild

Meetings Via Newsreels

I wondered
If I was
One of the relatively few
Children with my
Unresolved, confusing
War history

But old newsreels reminded me
I used to be
One of too many
Myriad, abandoned
Starved faces
From that time
And place

Were their wounds
Also adequately patched
Did kind families find them?

Was each one
Luckily loved
Back to
A miraculously
Normalized life

Survivor Guilt

Abba, forgive me for surviving
Mother, father, grandparents, relatives
Forgive my years here
When your lives were much more dear

Claims

If / When
I speculate my adoptive parent
Was really my birth mother
I did call her Ma
Though told she's my aunt

Relatives
Brother, sister, cousin dear
Please recall
All the hints, the dynamics
The tears in the fabric
Of the story

Then may God with
His needle of time
Repair our quilted
Family epic
With His multi-hued
Threads of love

And may poetry
Be kind, be healing
And lead
To a comforted peace

Obits and Orbits – Revelations 21:4

When
They die

Their stories stop
In mid-plot

These could, should be resumed
By their loved ones, families
Friends, neighbors

For God's glory

Otherwise the many worlds
They touched
That touched them

May be destroyed forever
Lost, killed or moved away

And we the bereft
Would be left
Without ancestral ties
Orphaned on islands of death

O Lord, Savior
Please create
Another more heavenly city

Where violence, pain
Illness and tears
Don't exist any more
For them

And help us build and keep
Inclusive sanctuaries
Of peace and faith here

Though after death's tragedies

These positives can
Never be quite
Comforting enough

Who Will Save Us?

Someone like
The savior of the *Altneushul* (Old-New Synagogue)
In Prague
That we all need

Cannot be a *golem*
Nor another
Super-powered action hero
Nor a manufactured robot
Nor any man-imagined creature

Is actually
Creator-God Himself become
Christ, the vicarious offering
Building the bridge
Over waters of death

Through Tears

With those tragedies to witness
Via true pictures, movies, books of awful times
How can I, a survivor, drift off to happy sleep
When the cries of the murdered still echo
Don't forget the effects of bloodthirsty hate

Though the warm humor of the Sholom Aleichem kind
Through earlier pogroms, smiles through tears,
Plays tunes for us on *shtetl* roofs

Yet, forgiveness shines from a tortured survivor's
obituary
Still, love's everlasting sun sings with the heart of my
heart
Don't forget the roses, the wonders God sends every
day
To treasure and keep company with the stones on the
graves

Holocaust Service at Agudas Achim

A hope of a homeland
A mourn of a chant
A sorrow bared, never ending
A refrain of never again

A ritual of remembrance
Shoah candles in a circle
Honoring millions of victims
Lit also for the ones who resisted

A time to pray to Thee, dear Abba, above
For Thy covering, co-suffering love

Deliver Us

Abba Shelanu, Our Father
Who art in heaven
Please deliver us
Protect and save us

From world-shaking macro evil
From constant micro greed
From ceaseless cruelty and selfishness
From the many cultures of hatred and death
On our planet

For Thine is the kingdom of love
Thine is the power of love
Thine is the glory of love

To Be Reborn

Why did so many survivors
Not want to share ancestry stories
Nor experiences harrowing
With their dear new-life families?

Maybe they didn't want to walk
In the same shoes as before
Nor claim the identities, commitments
Before the connection-breaking war

Maybe they feared picking up and carrying
The grim guilt of outlasting people gone
Reluctant to shadow golden lands of opportunity
Though repressed bitterness was passed on

How can those remaining victims
Keep their histories, yet be born again
Who can carry generational burdens
Except Jesus, God of love and salvation

Love Is the Main Miracle

It is a burden, this survivor guilt
Almost too heavy to bear
Is it false? Is it real?
Should my aching heart share?

Is life here a limited purgatory
That all persons must pass?
Can we be redeemed
If only we ask?

Jesus helps us carry the load
He is also salvation's road
The light of love above all
Be comforted, o my soul

After

Combining Psalm 23 and The Lord's Prayer

The Lord is our Shepherd
We shall not reject
Wisdom, peace, love, kindness, truth

The Lord is my Shepherd
I shall not dwell in deserts of bitterness
I shall not lack cooling waters of thankfulness

Our Father Who art in heaven
Glorified be Thy name
Not thrown aside, dishonored

Please protect us from viruses, enemies
Inside and outside
Deliver all from evil

Forgive us our trespasses
Keep us away from wrong roads, lies
And let us forever with Thee abide

Guarding a Language and Culture Shelter

It is important
It's defining

To shelter *Yiddishkeit*
To help this brave language,
This sage culture survive

It's also important
To testify about
Our individual journeys
To witness the graces given
To recognize and thank the Giver
To help with wise kindnesses, *mitzves*
Lovingly

Each in their own way
Let us pray

World Wars' Aftermath

After the wars
A long line of angels
Waited in the halls of heaven
Whispering secrets of peace
To creatures on earth

But few leaders
Could understand
Their old world language

While many regular folk
Concentrated on the pursuit
Of comforts' winking lights
This side of life

Whence and Whither?

Yiddish, *oy vey*, Yiddish
Where did you come from, where
Are you going?

Are you just a borrowing, cluttered language
Like some rooms in our house

Can you keep existing as such
And who will describe your poetry?

Is there a future in your past?
Oy, Yiddish, ven verst du
Vern a ladt, zein a mentsch
Azoi vee andere shprachen?

When will you
Become a regular
Cradle to age
Popular communicator
Like other languages?

Is There a Future in My Past?

Is there a future in my past?
Tell me, tea leaves of memories
Fortune-telling cookies

Uplifting sermons
And missed events of yesteryear
Political, pandemic
And destructive snow storms
Of previous months
While photos remain ungathered

How long, o Lord
After these questions
Will Thy graces last?

After the Holocaust

After the Holocaust
We wonder how
It could have happened

We proclaim never again
Can this be allowed

But Uighurs, and Rohingya
North Koreans, Asians, Syrians and countless others
Including schoolchildren trying to learn
Women denied rights
Races misjudged and mistreated
All those brethren
Were and are
Attacked and persecuted
Again and again

And we ourselves have been misled
And we can realize more clearly now

How blame games developed
Into genocide
Before

Here and Now

Lord, please help us, how
At this time and place, why
God please save us because
We can't rescue ourselves
We see sadly here and now

Lord of love,
Re-mind our minds
Re-heart our hearts
Re-birth our spirits
Comfort our souls

Through the wild wilderness of our thoughts
Within caves of endless worries
Lord, Thou canst visit in person

To present and discuss
Thy good news
About redemption and salvation

Betwixt and Between

If I could compartmentalize
Rationalize

One box would be
Filled with forever mourning
Justifiably, bitterly
For cruelty's victims

Another box would be
Lit with grateful smiles, songs
Declaring God is good
All the time

Could we, should we, dare we
Open both compartments
At once

After all
Smiling sunshine and frowning clouds
Are not always
Strictly shut into
Separate areas

Ghettoized

Islands

Islands of lights on waters of night
Bands of colors deep and bright
Keep us, o Lord, in Thy kind sight
Set this beautiful, yearning world right

As Long As We Live

As Long As We Live

Lessons to learn, day to befriend
Places to live in, people to see
Ways to mend, prayers to send
God to worship thankfully

Please Keep

Reconstitute us, Lord
Protect, revive us
Reform all those cells and nuclei
In our once innocent DNA
That resided in each world, person
Every galaxy and nation

Whatever was beautiful, truthful and good
Please keep and
Give a star or at least a planet
Sheltered by Thy Loving Holy Spirit

Help Us, Dear God

Be present in the present
Live beyond the past
Walk with Thee, Lord
Who all outlasts

And, on every road, help us
Sing poems about moments, stages and years
Say prayers for all continually
For Thy glory

Please strengthen us to
Witness with caring missions and ministries
The rest of our time here

Witnessing to Our Cells

Every cell is a beating heart
Wanting love, care, nourishment
Searching, looking for God
To be its protector and friend

Let us each tell our cells
To have one singing goal
To get together in a choir
Giving to God one whole soul

Skylight

Although
Our material and spiritual tents
Are fraying, swaying, greying

And
Even the present campsite is becoming
More bothered, cluttered

Often with
Negative winds, illnesses stronger
Than positive thoughts

Yet
Look through
The opened skylight

To see where later
We'll dance in the sunshine
Of His love beyond the stars

Now let's pray in the rains, the pains
Future fears, troubling signs
In faith that

We will forever
Rejoice together
With loved ones, mentors

Hearing the welcoming sounds
Of God's homecoming bands
Hallelujahs sung and refound

Getting There

Getting old
Is not a punishment

Becoming weaker
Is not a sin

Losing standing
In the workworld

Could be the beginning
Of an important part
Of a commissioned
Almost completed journey

As we review
Steps and ties
Our families, histories

As we perceive
God's holy light
Shining always higher
Ever deeper
And lovelier

Pattern in the Patchwork

Patchwork the quilt
Of ages, of stages
Though from far above
They form a pattern of love

From here we see the pilgrimage
Stop, start and change
Confusingly, frustratingly
While milestones sing nostalgically

Repeating - O what a blissful
Beautiful garden was this
Where and why has it been left
What is the next step

Even when pieces can be sown
Into some sort of covering or wall art
Who will keep it from tearing apart

Except Thou, o Lord
With Thy loving eye and caring hand
Who ties together all patches and lands

Reasons

Had wanted
To help those six million and more
Be honored
Some way, somehow

Now I
Care mainly for one
For family

A few cherished reasons, missions
To have been rescued, to pray
To keep following through
Every day anew

Caregiving Clues

Every needed skill whispers
Cloistered clues of caregiving

This has to be done before that
Don't be distracted, too slow or too fast

To hear God's voice
When the day's routines start

What's Wise At This Point

We're walking a fine line
Actually several that
Intersect confusingly while
We're treading water and
Trying to balance, prioritize

Different health issues
Keep moving goal posts of coping
With changeable prescriptions, diets, schedules
As old age demands its dues

God Will

Who will care for the caregiver?
God will
He is still
The Constant Responder

Rose At Christus Santa Rosa Hospital

Sweet little winking rose
Nestled within
The trimmed twigs
Of the landscaped entrance

Are you the namesake flower
Of Christus Santa Rosa Hospital
Encouraging in sign and nature
Promising help, hopefully cures

Window At Warm Springs Rehab

Pale blue the day's
Sky

White the snowy clouds
Drift by

The toy cars run around
To and fro

The palm branch hands
Wave languidly

Brown the small butterfly lonely
Reaches the 3rd story rehab window

Where we are

At This Moment

At this moment
Solitude clings
Like a suede cape
Like rolls of puffy
Absorbent cotton

In this hospital room
With a wooden
Crucifix on the wall

And my suffering Milo in bed
Sleeping away the sorrow
Of another aging calvary

Grateful For

Amazing, caring healthgivers
Diligent and knowledgeable
Skilled at managing
Diseases and time

Opening windows of hope
For multiple individuals
Each with urgent calls

What's Going On

Another Stage, Another World

It's a different life, world
Though the closet contents keep
Waving flags of familiarity
With obliging clothes of high hopes

Sighing in this twirled climate, halted habits
That they never had a chance
To honor spring, summer, fall
Of unprepared 2020

While we're going back
To what we missed in infanthood
Focused and loving baths, dressing,
Noting, celebrating with caregivers

Every good step

Pandemic Epic

We in San Antonio
And all over this, our laden world
Made closer
In our Covid suffering
Are waiting through
This pandemic epic

Now ten and counting
Months long gone
Of groundhog days
Melting into each other

Not even hibernating bears
Stay that long
In their cave bubbles

Between the Gold and Green

Between the gold and green seasons
Thanksgiving recalled, Christmas readiness

In this blurred year, hidden behind masks
Heeding melancholy reasons for distancing

Compromising by gathering
For welcome garage events

Echoing the missing holidays
With grateful green and gold layers
Of goodwill songs and talks shared

Whom Do We Call?

We sighed through it
We cried through it
Tragically many died from it

This year-long pandemic

For comfort and protection
We cooked, renovated, practiced skills and distancing
Made quilts and new foods, wore masks
We visited hospitals, wrote a little, studied a little
Zoomed in and out of meetings
Wondering how and when
Schools and offices and churches
Restaurants and theaters, stores and more
Would re-open for good
And when
We could be closer again

Some countries reasoned their collective escape
From this cruel plague
With restrictive but necessary protocols
Others claimed their people's individual
Freedom from health rules
To follow leaders cruel

But the virus sailed on
With improved variations
It wanted to conquer also

And now, what do we know?
What do we fear
From this new year?

Whom do we call
In this unforeseen time stall?
May it be God,
Protector of all

For Strange Weather – Providentially

These are fine things
I remarked to myself
Once given or bought
Truly welcome just now

A beautiful woollen Bavarian sweater
(They know winter)
A heavier than usually warranted
Embroidered blanket
Thin, yet warming driving gloves

All and more
Waiting around the house
In our sunny southwest city
Hoping to be appreciated
Eventually

This week a bizarre
Cold front blackout
Showed me just why
These wintry, wonderful goods
Were granted, found
Happily

And through many winnowings
Were kept and conserved
Providentially

Quarantines Multiplied

Now we are
Many times quarantined

By winter storms
Power failures
Aging weaknesses
Not to forget
The world-wide viruses

And we finally realize
We have been leading
Privileged, electric lives

Cold and in the dark
Let's appreciate
What we once had

Surprised Landscape

Surprise, surprise
I didn't realize
Snow in the yard,
The roofs, branches
Could look so cute

White bonnet sits
On the top level
Of our little patio fountain

Arbor vitae come into their own
Identities as Christmas trees
Flocked with white
Standing bright

Sporting wintry patterns through grills
Iron lattice chairs, back yard fence chill
All totally astonishing
For San Antonio, usually tropical

And now, next day
Another snow globe of a scene
Outside the windows

With white flurries hurried by
An invisible hand
That pushes the wind
Heralding a portal
To another dimension

…Does Narnia exist after all?

Was It a (Collective) Dream?

How lovely the piano concert
Of ever loved musicals bestowing
Warmth on cold evenings

New recipes for the freezing weather
And multiple taquerias discovered,
Card games, readings

To celebrate electricity-less
Collective hibernating
A snow fort and
Snow figures still trying to stand

Reminders of a fleeting
Mystical fantasy land
In bewildered San Antonio

Perhaps soon
The daily, many-miracled
Newspaper may wait in the driveway

To tell us how we did
With the four-day blackout

New Clothes for Plants

After a state-wide, strange
White blanketed week
Up and down the street
And on our front lawn

Small, chunky sabal palms
Plus other tropical plants
Glow bright orange
Strangely celebratory
Temporarily

As if costumed for
A happy Mardi Gras parade
That they missed

Because of this year's
Protocols for
Our world-wearied pandemic

Another Storm

Thunderstorms with sides of tornadoes
Rolled into
Our tv evening
On trapezoid-diagrammed wagons
With wheels of hail, horses of lightning

Then rumbled out into the distance
The warned windows
Sighed with relief

What Old Normal?

What is the
Not-so-long-ago
Old normal?

Is it before the freak winter storm
In our southwestern city
Of San Antonio
A week ago
Halting power, light, warmth, water

Or is it before that
A year ago
When we still hadn't heard
Of Covid, anti-viral masks
Social distancing
And were making multiple plans
With family, friends, acquaintances

Or was it even before that
Three years ago
When falls were rare, get-togethers often
Languages with meet-up groups practiced weekly
I still shopped frequently (maybe addictively)
We exercised and swam in the gym
Refreshingly

Or is it even before that
Five years ago
We scurried out of the house
With schedules
For church, teaching, substituting

Lord, tell us what returning
Old normal to wish for, to pray for
Realistically

Stops and Starts

On a Dappled Road

Stops and starts
How to see through the clouds
On hope's dappled road

Looking back
Trying not to turn
Into a nostalgic figure of salt

Passing buildings, places
Holding memories
Turned inside out

Continuing without maps
Into future forests
Around bends unknown

Time's aging voice
Whispers warnings
Becomes a constant goad

Dawn Haiku

To get up early
And watch God lovingly paint
Today's horizons

In Pursuit of Reprieves

I took three precious
Hours from sleep
To look for my lost watch
To make sure that these life minutes
Aren't ticking away unnoticed

God charitably
Helped me locate that compass

And rediscover His road
Even while pursuing
Heavenly reprieves
Above numbering dials

Powers of Mistaken Numbering

Hidden dimensions
Lurk in mistaken typing
Of numbers less than true
Take me back, sadly or smiling
Nostalgically

Whereas
Numbers added
Zoom me forward, imagining
The next day
Year or decade

Fearfully or hopefully
Venturing in cloud lands new

Much is Moot

Towards the end of
This semi-colon life
Much is moot

Moot the movement
Moot the steps
Moot the regrets
Moot the conundrums of identity
Moot the scheduling bets

Though eternal
The soul's love

And God Who can repurpose
And redeem mistakes
Helping us along
The real road
To His everlasting, wonderful, joyful
Heavenly kingdom

Desert Pauses

Oy vey, this trudging in the desert
Dreary the journey … yet, wait
There's a flaming bush
That Moses had known about before
With his princely education of yore

Suddenly however, at that place of awe
This was a curiosity to behold
Then God spoke

He speaks every time
We stop amazed at any wonder
To ponder the work of the Creator

First He Said

Take your shoes off
Those soles of your soul
That step on the sad ground
Carelessly, pragmatically
Following causality

Meditate on what astounds
And you and I will discuss
Miracles and see
What's lost can be found
And we'll wonder as one.

Previous Promising Projects

Clutter creating buried cities
Each with its promised projects and sheltered secrets
Each covered by sands of time
All needing an archeologist
And better housekeeper
To restore their landmarks and signs

While I wander without enough energy
Squandering limited minutes helplessly
Needing Christ's organizational economies
And prayers for my aging, tired ADD

Though

Though I have bonds and debts
With pots and purses and stuff galore
Yet God sends psalms on dove's wings
Reflecting silver and gold
From His heavenly shores

It's Possible

You can make everything a rosary
Or a bouquet of flowers for the Father
Each gift calling forth new blooms and beads
Of thanks to God
Who suffered to be your Savior

You can build an altar
In the garden of your soul, your heart's mansion
To God who gave you so many blessings
And love, life, work, joys, family, home
And wondrous salvation

Support

As we age in place
In this flexible, supportive house that we love
That you found, that you furbished,
Organized and supplied
Just right

We think of you, love you, thank you
Every minute
Dear son, dear daughter, cherished grandchildren
Forever our lights

There Are, There Were

Dear ones, friends, acquaintances,
There are, there were

Sunrises and sunsets
Homes and harbors
Pauses and journeys

While our mutual Father, Savior
Walked with us,
Always prays with us
Through gravity's tests

Day's Beginnings

Baby-blue filtering through
Dark blue black-out curtains
How lovely your silent footsteps
In the still sleeping air

Molecules slowly meeting other
Objects' configurations
Trying to cushion the sound
In the careful morning

Four, no – five, no – six, no – seven
Light sources in my yellow-painted room
How considerate your patient readiness
For older projects, new poems

Is All That Weight Needed

Take away my baggage, Lord
I prayed as I shlepped some
Heavy moods to another room
With another view

Hot Summer Day

Black dog mood
Pick up that pencil
Decorated with
Glittering multi-colored notes

And be wise
And realize
God and His angels
People and signs

Are always talking to you
Encouraging you
Alleviating

The dog-day
Summer afternoon
Blues

To Patch the Time-Space Gaps

The blank afternoon
Plays a melancholy
Minor key tune

That tries to patch
Musically
The time-space gaps
With notes and rests

While I
Caress my soul-mate napping
Write, type, organize poems
Tend to health and house matters
Read a sadder biography

Some sweet ice-cream beckons
And some potent HTP
To re-supply some serotonin

Finally and before all else
Should be sending
Prayers to God who cares
What we do with our rescued selves
And time-space gaps
That need darning

At the End of the Day

The day has crumbled
Into small cookie pieces
Let me present its minutes
Back to Thee, Lord
For better bread

Invitation to Dreams

Silvery river within
A heavenly green forest
Where clouds roam calmly

Hopes

A string of diamonds
Lighting our near horizons
Windows presented

Around Every Corner

At Each Bend, Around Every Corner

At each bend
Find questions, advice
Signs and missions of love

Around every corner
Prayers and praise
To God, our dear Father, send

Archeologists

The student diggers
In a long-ago cohort
Are all dead or aging

Who will be the archeologists
Finding, cataloguing, stewarding
The artifacts of our lives?

Who will count how old our souls are?
And if our ministries really reached far?

Hospital Stay During Pandemic

Why are you so far, dear Milo, though so near
Where we can't see you, hug you, reassure you
That you aren't alone while fighting bravely
Against age-old sufferings and new pains?

We so long to help you, witness health workers
Hold out olive branches of hope to you and to us
And ask God to strengthen you to minister some more
In your own individualistic sweet way

Five Years' Difference

Five years ago, you were hiking
With son and grandson in New Mexico mountains
Driving with daughter revisiting your ancestral city
Still teaching, editing, exercising, singing

Five years ago, five years ago
What will we be like five years from now?
How will we be living, coping with aging somehow
Resting, reminiscing more, still praying

And Now

What to do about not substituting?
Not having any stories
About school excursions

Yet so many home layers
Of discussing, caring, learning, visiting
Writing, organizing, cleaning

But nothing to twitter about
Gossip about
Advertise about

Except to be proud
About short
Mainly medical outings

While wishing everyone well

Any Choice Made, Any Words Said

Is it helpful?
Is it kind?
It it rational and wise?
Is it with a good attitude?
Towards God, towards others?

Is it merciful?
Is it fair?
Is it just?
Is it creative, yet focused?

Is it in God's benevolent will?
Is it with the help
Of God's loving Holy Spirit?

Politically Useful

It could have been me
But for God's grace
You have our
Thoughts and prayers

Is that appropriate to say, to commiserate
About someone's tragic event?

Or a little glib?
Triumphalist? Ableist?

Do those cliches
Show much love
For our not so fortunate neighbors?

Or are those just
The superficially sorry
The politically useful
Things to say?

Unending Questions

Truth or truthiness?

Faith in the absolutely best
Of Plato's ideal forms
In heaven's pure sphere above
Or confidence in our own
Searching, finding
Benevolently using
Reason

Or is it all relative?

What's perfect for the moment
For every individual
In each ocean
Steering, driven, or floating
On a different boat

What to rely on or respect
If all is deemed just picturesque?

How to wrestle with such choice
As you did,
Dear Adam, dear Eve?
And what about us
Your descendants?

Possible?

Wouldn't it be lovely to be told
There is something better than gold
That is waiting for us around the bend
That will bring glad news and sorrows mend?

Wouldn't it be nice if we could hear
All God tells us loud and clear
To love our neighbors and pray for their souls
To care for nature and fulfill commissioned roles?

Wouldn't it be amazing if we could walk
With God 's Spirit not only as we talk the talk?
And meditate mindfully on God's holy word
Ever learning, to good deeds stirred

For Such a Time as This – Influence of *Jane Eyre* by Charlotte Bronte

Jane Eyre, how eerie
That, at fifteen, I
So thrilled at that
Beautiful ending to
The lovely novel
Even with the fifteenth
(or more) reading

For, its romantic message
Nestled in my soul and
Now guides and lights
This home-care-giving
Aging stage

Abba, how did You know
(Of course You knew)
What comfort, what helping passion
We would need
Even before we met
So many years ago

What Will It Take?

What
Dance of molecules
Gives us the power-point display
Of the awakening dawn
The dark blue sky quickly changing
To a powder blue calling
Through still sleeping blinds?

What
Symphony of atoms
Sends us lunar eclipses
Twilight's comforting shawl
Rainbow colors deepening to
Darkened bejeweled purples
Numinous pauses
Waiting for our responses?

What
Will it take
To shake us into amazement?
Beholding God's works of beauty
To believe in love and salvation

Who can awaken us
O Savior, except Thou?
Please reach us Lord, somehow

Who Do You Think?

Who do you think you are?
Asked Joseph's brothers
Are you the favorite child or star
That we should follow you?

Who do you think I am?
Jesus asked His disciples
Peter declared – You are the Lord,
Our Master, Rabbi and the Son of Man

Who does he think he is?
Said the scorners about Christ
Is He the king of the Jews?
Is He the new Messiah?

Who do you think you are?
God asks each and every one
And answers – A bright and shining person
An essential part of Creation

Let's Be Advised

Everyone Can

Everyone can write a note
To God
And put it on
Their private wailing wall

Preparing For Shoah Remembrance

Taste
The saddened smiles
Through tears

Go back
To commemorate
The tragedies
Of victims

At least
Three months
Of the surviving year

Between Gravity and Grace – After Simone Weil

Appreciate, meditate
On the physics of objects
Weight and gravity
Color and placement
Light and shadow

To move more slowly
Through a spiritual portal
To the beyond

To find yourself
Suddenly transported
Into a peaceful land
Of poetry
And grace

Surely on the Shores

Worried and weary
Write a poem

When signs portend more illness at night
Remember moments of healing light

Wrestling with insomnia's syndrome
Let words on paper roam

Surely on the shores of wonder
You'll find seashell signs from your Creator

With messages of energizing grace
From your never sleeping Savior

Through Different Idioms

Capture the new language but let it flow
Over the grids of what we know
Gaze at the birds, but let them fly
In fields of clouds, through windy skies

Harness the ocean, but don't harm the waters
So finely orchestrated by God the Father
Descend to deep springs of childhood neuroses
Then thank God for His healing gracious

Let me tell my flippant thoughts
To focus on prayer and devotions as taught
By our Father in heaven who is our Rabbi on earth
And speaks through our idioms His mentoring word

The Grateful Side – Luke 5:4-6; John 21:6

Cast the net
On the right side
Of your ship

Then you will find
Glittering multitudes of fish

More than your
Nets can easily hold

Cast your thoughts
On the right side
The grateful side
Of your soul

Then you will find
Surprizing gifts

More than your
Memory or prayer
Nets can hold

If Ever

If ever could improve
I must be born again for good
Let neurons' negative habits
(Under construction since childhood)
Make way for God's Holy Spirit

Wisely, Happily

Moods and dimensions
Sun and moontime
Wake and sleepland
Practical and spiritual
Imaginary and sense-perceived

Thoughts of present, future and past
Given by God
To be balanced wisely
To make our blessed journeys last
And continued happily

Out of Boxes

Games give you challenging boxes
Though never
Can you ever
Move beyond their dimensions

Of their exciting premises
And competitive limits

Reading, writing, art, learning
Take you out of the boxes
To develop your own possibilities
Offering wisdom of others' thoughts

To travel beyond
Your experiences, situations
With new journeys
Through God's awesome creation

Let's Be Creative And

Make a crown out of time's diamonds
Weave a macrame cloak out of words
Dance with the music of the Holy Spirit
Sing our thanks to our good Lord

Paint mind pictures of glad thoughts
Build witnessing mansions
Construct bridges of hope for all
Proclaim His beautiful eternal salvation

Advertising Advice

When you hear advice
From inside, from outside
Your mind

Is it God's wise voice?
Is it kind, is it caring?
Does it honor Him?

Or is it an algorithm
Calculating and cynical
Leading you astray
For corporate profit?

Unintended Consequences

Don't break the dishes
In your hurry
To clear the house

Don't lose the baby
As you're throwing out
Used bath water

Don't push God away
Because of your questions
About traditional doctrines

Don't step on love's delicate shawl
Trying to make others march
Into a righteous future

Those dreams of a just utopia
Can so easily become dystopic

Don't offend God
By taking up for Him
Arms of criticism

As you live with people, creation
Also dwell in God's realm
Of love from above

Biculturally, amazedly
Prayerfully, mercifully

Hope for the best
That others be protected
Well led and blessed

Healthier

Bitter flowers
In your mind

Throw them away
Another day

God will give you
A sweeter bouquet

The Comfort of Studies – After Simone Weil

Academic work for young, for lifelong students
Should be so enjoyed, so prioritized
That, as a pearl of great price,

This treasure is always
Worthwhile to pursue, to acquire
Its gifts and comforts that instruct, that inspire
And forever keep on giving

Thirst Quenching, Nourishing

First, the Bible, the well that never runs dry
Then you can turn to so many wise written works
That give insights, form helpful ideas

That labor with God, the Redeemer
Of hurts and quandaries
To create positive nourishment

To throw artisan breads on rivers of lives
While curiously specialized
And timed for individual needs
To heal each soul with divine encounters

And Let's

Let's give meaning
To the fallen leaves

Let's find reason and art
In everyday vistas and artifacts

Let's understand the why and how
Of histories then and politics now

Let's pray for near and far neighbors
And talk with our co-suffering Creator

Send

As, after typing e-mails, we hit send
Let all our prayers end with Amens

Multiple Mercies

Abide With Empathy

To comfort and protect
To manage quality
Time for you
To abide gladly

To bring empathy to bear
In tandem with Jesus
As through the years
Caring we've shared

Carried

A child carried in the rain
By his sheltering father
Is happy to be content
In snug, loving safety

A worshipper carried through pain
By the caring, transcendent Father
Keeps believing because of mercies
Cooling comforts sent mysteriously

If / When

If / when
Your children disobey
Make mistakes
Go their own bold way

Don't you still love them
Unconditionally?

Your Abba, Father
Knows your trespasses

Yet came to earth
To walk, talk with you
To forgive you

And to love you
Eternally

Eat, Drink, Remember, Honor

Honor the Passover
Your journey
To God's country
Of milk and honey

Remember God's works with symbols

The unleavened bread of hurry
The bitter herbs of desert adversity
The egg of renewed life
The shankbone of sacrifice
The wine of promise
The dessert mixture
A metaphor for the mortar
Once used for building projects

All that is now needed
To keep living with Passover history

Dayenu
(It Is Enough For Us)

You know it's from God
If, whatever you receive after seeking,
Is enough, but not too much

If strange mercies surprize with
Their perfect timing

If gifts of grace
Fulfill His redemptive will
And relieve the weary, fearful heart

Generational Wonders

With wonderful support
Considering our comfort
You refurbish, renew our house
That you found a while ago
For us

To protect our bodies and hopes
You carpet our todays and tomorrows
Install on the walls steadying grab bars

You transplant storage with another chest of drawers
Give multiple helps to our disheveling lives
To keep rollating, breathing along

Transportation, shopping, check-in calls
Food prepared and brought, visits and sharing
Curtains, more shelves, books and supplies
Lift chair, exercisers, better viewing screens
Projects inspired and cares eased

How marvelous are your many gifts
Dear family
Forever treasured givers

Photographs Become Stars

Certain significant moments
The mind recollects

Into long-term memory albums
That never, o never leave
The photographs become
Insightful stars

That enlighten
Edify and revive
Times past,
Days now

Celebration

Already in February
Of next year

The chairs on the patio
Stay still in their nostalgic
Conversational configuration

For our 50th anniversary

A lovely commemoration
Of a happy celebration

Lent

Flowers and plants gifted
At multiple occasions
For encouragement meant

A beautiful link lent
Between outside and inside spaces
The natural and the architectural

For loving couples
For children and parents
For family, hosts, guests and friends

Connections, communications
Commemorations, confirmations
Eden to earth
Sent

Right There

What
Multiple treasures
Right on the streets

Diamonds
Of the dawn's dew

Silver
Pebbles shine

Gold
Beams ushering evening

Emerald
Greenery encouraging

Ruby, sapphire
Spring flowers

Jewelry
Just as colorful
As you'd ever see

So why sigh
For metals below ground

When God gives us enough
Daily decorations
Right on the streets

Signs and Texts

Wonders upon wonders
Why can't we perceive
The forests that breathe
The clear glass of sand
Reflecting His majesty

Signs and texts
God sends with sparkles of gold
Written in a heavenly alphabet
Whose language we learn slowly
As we are made whole

To Thank God

It was
A good day
Mostly

Week-long worry
About prescription resolved
Temporarily

Gold and red fall-painted
Tips of trees
Reflecting the afternoon sun
Up and down the street

A nervous medical excursion
Now realized possible
With a traffic light sweet

Thought-provoking conversations
With Milo, renewing routine followed
Lovingly

Pushing away
Feared future days
Persistently

Thanking God
As often as should recall
Openly and privately
Sincerely

Whose Gift?

Reappeared today
An ancient memory

Lacing white and silver
Ice-skates in a
Hot-chocolate warmed
Snack bar

Gliding out clumsily
Happily
On a park rink

But I don't remember
Who bought or gave
That moving present

Did I ever thank them?

Was it a gift? Sacrifice?

To Catch a Bluebird

Happiness
For one, for several
Or for many

Cannot be pursued
Grimly

As a colorful bird
Warbling in a sheltering tree
Should not be caged alive

Nor can it be completely
Identified

But often
It sings messages and tidings
Anonymously

Rebekah At the Well – Synchronicity – Genesis 24: 1-67

For you He had to move the universe

To grant your prayers for particular matters
For great or small needs,
Helpful or life-saving mercies
For a person, time and space
To appear together
At just the right place

But where and how does free will play into
Those undeniable miracles and undeserved graces?

Love, Especially

He Is Here

He is here to guide
Through every grief

What better messiah
Than one who could forgive

As well as conquer
Death to be our Savior

Where else is the well
For all our thirst

Where else dwells truth and light
Besides with His word

On All Levels

The horizontal and the vertical
A cross of forgiveness
On all levels

A death we are not fit to describe
For what can our fallen surfer thoughts judge
Except to our Redeemer all confide

Liberation

As she lay dying
With loving words
She liberated me

I pray that
I can borrow the key of kindness
And help free someone else
From unfair chains

Of assumed guilt

Heralding

Will our one and only earth
Its once finely balanced nature
Ever be restored

Thereby heralding, modelling
God's forgiving redemption

Happily, Harmoniously

Happily, harmoniously
Holding hands here
Let us worship God together
Praising Him forever

Where Found

Books rest as objects
Until they open a universe
Where we can discuss with the author
In an I-Thou world of words

Art removes fortresses, masks
Showing new views of reality or imagination
As well as the heart of the artist
Otherwise cocooned and vulnerable

Love sings its just-born and repeated poems
Dances to anti-gravity tunes
Builds homes and havens,
Then steps out
To find a ladder, to meet God together

Every Day an Adventurous Journey

It's another part so blessed
Of our forever love story

It's a daily journey, adventure
Twenty-four/seven togetherness

Towards

My dearest love
Granted for a lifetime here
We have travelled over
Landscapes, learning mindscapes
Together, weathering
Many stages

And now in smaller spaces
Of healing rooms shared
Bounded by concerned care
Comforting each other

We move slowly
Towards God's eternal
Divine love